STARS in the SPOTLIGHT

Molly O'Mara

New York

Published in 2007 by The Rosen Publishing Group, Inc.
29 East 21st Street, New York, NY 10010

Copyright © 2007 by The Rosen Publishing Group, Inc.

All rights reserved. No part of this book may be reproduced in any form without permission in writing from the publisher, except by a reviewer.

Book Design: Haley Wilson

Photo Credits: Cover, pp. 6, 14, 18 © Frank Micelotta/Getty Images; p. 4 © Stephen Shugerman/Getty Images; p. 8 © Mark Mainz/Getty Images; p. 10 © Kevin Winter/Getty Images; p. 12 © Newsmakers; p. 16 © Carlos Alverez/Getty Images; p. 20 © Frederick M. Brown/Getty Images; p. 22 © Andrew H. Walker/Getty Images; p. 24 © Getty Images/Getty Images; p. 26 © Carlo Allegri/Getty Images; p. 28 © Dave Hogan/Getty Images.

Library of Congress Cataloging-in-Publication Data

O'Mara, Molly.
  Beyoncé / Molly O'Mara.
     p. cm. -- (Stars in the spotlight)
  Includes index.

ISBN: 978-1-4358-3831-4

  1. Knowles, Beyoncé--Juvenile literature. 2. Singers--United States--Biography--Juvenile literature. I. Title. II. Series.
  ML3930.K66O43 2006
  782.42164'092--dc22
  [B]
                            2006016918

Manufactured in the United States of America

Contents

Meet Beyoncé	5
Young Performer	7
Star Search	9
Taking a Chance	11
Destiny's Child	13
More Success	15
Songwriter of the Year	17
On Her Own	19
The 2004 Grammy Awards	21
Movie Star!	23
Together Again	25
Beyoncé's Other Interests	27
Reaching Out to Others	29
In the Future	30
Glossary	31
Index	32
Web Sites	32

Meet Beyoncé

Millions around the world know Beyoncé Knowles just as Beyoncé. She began her **professional** career as a singer in the popular group Destiny's Child. Beyoncé has found that she is interested in many other parts of the entertainment world. She is now also a songwriter, actress, and fashion designer. Beyoncé has done all this at a young age. What will she do next? Anything she wants to do! In this book, you'll read how hard work and great talent helped Beyoncé to become one of the most famous entertainers in the world!

Beyoncé has won many awards for her singing. Here she is shown at the 2006 Grammy Awards.

Young Performer

Beyoncé was born on September 4, 1981, in Houston, Texas. Although she began entertaining at a young age, she remembers being afraid to perform at her first school talent show. However, as soon as she heard the music, her fears disappeared. After that, Beyoncé enrolled in dance school and sang in her church choir. She began going to many singing and dancing contests. She won thirty-five local talent competitions in a row!

Beyoncé made some important friends when she was young. These friends were LaTavia Roberson, LeToya Luckett, and Kelly Rowland. The four friends often sang together around Houston.

Beyoncé calls herself "Sasha" when she performs on stage. "Sasha" is not afraid to perform in front of a crowd.

Star Search

Beyoncé and the other girls in the singing group were only 10 and 11 years old when they started. Everyone knew they had a lot of talent, though! They decided to send a videotape of themselves singing to a television show called *Star Search*. *Star Search* was a show on which different people could compete against each other for prizes. Beyoncé's group was invited to be on the show!

Beyoncé and her friends performed well but didn't win *Star Search*. Beyoncé said they learned that talent wasn't enough. They had to "become more serious" and work harder to be successful.

Beyoncé kept dreaming that she would one day perform for millions of people. Here she is on MTV's *Total Request Live* with singer Jessica Simpson and host Damien Fahey.

Taking a Chance

After Beyoncé and her friends appeared on *Star Search*, Beyoncé's father, Matthew, believed even more in the girls' dream to become professional singers. He decided to quit his job to help the girls become famous. The family struggled with money for several years.

The group practiced every day. In the summers, they started each morning by exercising and singing at the same time. They had vocal and dance coaches, too. They also watched videos of famous singers such as Whitney Houston, Michael and Janet Jackson, and Tina Turner. While they waited for their big chance, they worked hard to be even better.

Matthew Knowles asked different record companies to help Beyoncé's group. Here he is with Beyoncé at the 2004 Grammy Awards.

Destiny's Child

Beyoncé's group eventually called itself Destiny's Child. They were signed by Columbia Records in 1996. The record company helped the singers record their songs and sell their records.

In 1998, the group put out an album called *Destiny's Child*. It featured a song called "No, No, No" that reached number 1 on the **R&B/Hip-Hop** charts. Their second album came out the next year. *The Writing's on the Wall* included "Say My Name," "Jumpin', Jumpin,'" and "Bills, Bills, Bills." Destiny's Child was now a three-person group that included Beyoncé, Kelly Rowland, and Michelle Williams.

Kelly (left), Beyoncé, and Michelle (right) pose after hearing they were nominated for two Grammy Awards in 2001. "Say My Name" won two Grammy Awards, including Best R&B Song. Beyoncé helped write this song.

More Success

People were impressed with Destiny's Child's singing and dancing abilities. They could blend their voices into beautiful harmonies. While they sang, they danced with exact **choreographed** moves. They always put on a great show together. Their many fans wanted to see and hear more from this group.

Destiny's Child released their second top-selling album in 2001. This one was called *Survivor*. The song "Survivor" won a 2002 Grammy Award for Best R&B Performance by a Duo or Group. The song "Independent Women Part 1" was used in the movie *Charlie's Angels*. Both songs are about strong women seeking success—just like Beyoncé, Kelly, and Michelle!

Here Michelle (left), Beyoncé, and Kelly (right) perform at the Verizon Ladies First Tour in 2004.

Songwriter of the Year

Beyoncé won a special award in 2001. The American Society of **Composers**, Authors, and Publishers named her Songwriter of the Year for her work with Destiny's Child. Beyoncé was only the second woman ever to win this honor. She was also the first African American woman to receive it.

After their third album, the members of Destiny's Child decided they each wanted to work on their own projects for a while. Beyoncé had been helping to produce many of the songs for Destiny's Child. Now she had the chance to create a **solo** album.

The women of Destiny's Child are great friends and support each other's solo projects.

On Her Own

In 2002 and 2003, Beyoncé worked with some famous singers. She helped create a hit song with rapper Jay-Z called "'03 Bonnie and Clyde." She also sang a remake of the song "The Closer I Get to You" with **legendary** performer Luther Vandross. Beyoncé later won another Grammy for this song.

Beyoncé released her first solo album, *Dangerously in Love*, in 2003. She again worked with Jay-Z on a song called "Crazy in Love." Beyoncé sang with **reggae** artist Sean Paul in the song "Baby Boy." Both songs became top hits.

Beyoncé and Jay-Z's "Crazy in Love" was number 1 on the music charts for several weeks. Here Beyoncé and Jay-Z arrive at the 2004 MTV Video Music Awards.

The 2004 Grammy Awards

Beyoncé's solo album sold over 4 million copies in the United States and over 8 million around the world. It was the sixth best-selling album in the United States in 2003. Not only did fans love her work, but the music **critics** loved it, too. In 2004, Beyoncé won five Grammy Awards.

By 2003, Beyoncé had also explored another area of entertainment as an actress. She played the role of Carmen in a TV movie for MTV called *Carmen: A Hip Hopera*. This movie's plot was based on the famous nineteeth-century opera *Carmen*. The words and music were rewritten for an **audience** that enjoys hip-hop.

The five Grammy Awards Beyoncé won in 2004 tied the most ever given to a female singer in a single year.

Movie Star!

After *Carmen: A Hip Hopera*, Beyoncé became interested in more acting projects. She costarred with Mike Myers in the 2002 film *Austin Powers in Goldmember*. Her character, Foxxy Cleopatra, showed that Beyoncé could be funny as well as act in serious roles. The film made more money than any other **comedy** ever!

Two more movies followed. Beyoncé had a starring role with Cuba Gooding Jr. in *The Fighting Temptations* in 2003. She also starred with comedian Steve Martin in *The Pink Panther* in 2006. In both of these roles, Beyoncé played characters with singing talent.

Here Beyoncé is shown with Steve Martin, her costar in *The Pink Panther*.

Together Again

After 3 years apart, Beyoncé, Kelly Rowland, and Michelle Williams decided to work together again as Destiny's Child. They released an album called *Destiny Fulfilled* in 2004. Some believe they chose this title because it was the group's final original album. *Destiny Fulfilled* includes many hits, such as "Lose My Breath," which Beyoncé cowrote.

In 2005, Destiny's Child toured and performed in over seventy cities around the world. So far, the group has sold more than 50 million albums. They released an album of their most popular songs in October 2005 called *#1's*.

At the 2005 World Music Awards, Destiny's Child received an award for selling more records than any other women's singing group in history.

Beyoncé's Other Interests

Singing, songwriting, and acting keep Beyoncé very busy, but not too busy for even more projects! Beyoncé and her mother, Tina, have always loved fashion. Tina creates most of the clothes worn by Beyoncé and Destiny's Child when they perform and make appearances at events. In 2005, Beyoncé and Tina started a clothing line so that all women could wear her **unique** clothes. They call the line House of Deréon (duh-RAY-ahn) after Beyoncé's grandmother, Agnes Deréon. Beyoncé and Tina work together to design the clothes. Tina says she uses Beyoncé's sense of style to inspire her work.

Beyoncé is shown here with her mother, Tina Knowles, who designs many of her daughter's dresses.

Reaching Out to Others

Beyoncé doesn't just use her fame to sell things. She also uses it to help people in need. Beyoncé and Kelly Rowland began a Houston community center called the Knowles-Rowland Center for Youth. This is a place for kids to meet, have a good time, and feel safe. Beyoncé also helped start the Survivor Foundation for people who lost their homes in 2005's Hurricane Katrina.

Beyoncé even found a way to use her songwriting talents for charity. She helped write the Destiny's Child song "Stand Up for Love." This song asks people to contribute to children's charities.

Here Beyoncé speaks to children in South Africa. Beyoncé often works with children's charities.

In the Future

Beyoncé has done so much already! She has won awards for her singing and songwriting. She has starred in hit movies. She has helped to create a clothing line. She works to help people in need. What will Beyoncé do next?

For now, Beyoncé is focused on her film career, but plans for another solo album are not far behind. Whatever she does, Beyoncé will never leave behind her love for music. How did she rise from an unknown talent to an R&B superstar? Just listen to Beyoncé's amazing voice and you'll know!

Glossary

audience (AW-dee-uhns) A group of people watching or listening to a performance.

choreographed (KOHR-ee-uh-grafd) Describing the planned movements that dancers make to music.

comedy (KAH-muh-dee) A story that is funny and has a happy ending.

composer (kuhm-POH-zuhr) Someone who writes music.

critic (KRIH-tihk) A person who makes or gives a judgment about the value, beauty, or quality of something.

hip-hop (HIP–HOP) A type of music and dance associated with rap music.

legendary (LEH-juhn-dair-ee) Very famous.

professional (pruh-FEH-shuh-nuhl) Done by a person who is paid for work involving a special skill.

R&B (AHR AND BEE) The shortened name of a style of music called rhythm and blues, a combination of blues and jazz.

reggae (RAY-gay) A style of music originally from Jamaica.

solo (SOH-loh) Being done by one person.

unique (yew-NEEK) Different from all others.

Index

A
actress, 5, 21
American Society of Composers, Authors, and Publishers, 17
Austin Powers in Goldmember, 23

C
Carmen: A Hip Hopera, 21, 23
Charlie's Angels, 15
Columbia Records, 13

D
Dangerously in Love, 19
Destiny Fulfilled, 25
Destiny's Child, 5, 13, 15, 17, 25, 27, 29
Destiny's Child, 13

F
fashion, 5, 27
Fighting Temptations, The, 23

G
Grammy Award(s), 15, 19, 21

H
House of Deréon, 27

J
Jay-Z, 19

K
Knowles-Rowland Center for Youth, 29

L
Luckett, LeToya, 7

M
Matthew, 11

P
Paul, Sean, 19
Pink Panther, The, 23

R
Roberson, LaTavia, 7
Rowland, Kelly, 7, 13, 15, 25, 29

S
solo album, 17, 19, 21, 30
Songwriter of the Year, 17
Star Search, 9, 11
Survivor, 15
Survivor Foundation, 29

T
Tina, 27

V
Vandross, Luther, 19

W
Williams, Michelle, 13, 15, 25
Writing's on the Wall, The, 13

Web Sites

Due to the changing nature of Internet links, PowerKids Press has developed an online list of Web sites related to the subject of this book. This site is updated regularly. Please use this link to access the list:
http://www.powerkidslinks.com/stars/beyonce/

www.ingramcontent.com/pod-product-compliance
Lightning Source LLC
Chambersburg PA
CBHW040326100526
44584CB00002BA/213